Turbulent Planet

Violent Skies
Hurricanes

EXPRESS EDITION

Chris Oxlade

Raintree

Chicago, Illinois

For information, address the Publishers:
Raintree, 100 N. LaSalle, Suite 1200, Chicago, IL 60602

Originated by Dot Gradations Ltd, UK
Printed and bound in China
10 09 08 07 06
10 9 8 7 6 5 4 3 2 1

Library of Congress Cataloging-in-Publication Data

Oxlade, Chris.
  Violent skies : hurricanes / Chris Oxlade.
     p. cm. -- (Turbulent planet)
  Includes bibliographical references and index.
  ISBN 1-4109-1737-1 (library binding-hardcover) --
  ISBN 1-4109-1747-9 (pbk.) 1. Hurricanes--Juvenile literature.
  I. Title. II. Series.
  QC944.2.O952 2005
  551.55'2--dc22
                                        2005006359

This leveled text is a version of Freestyle: Turbulent Planet: Violent Skies.

Acknowledgments

p.4/5, Frank Lane Picture Agency; p.5 top, Science Photo Library/NASA/Goddard Space Flight Center; p.5 middle, Corbis/Annie Griffiths Belt; p.5 bottom, Corbis/Jim McDonald; p.7, Science Photo Library/Carl Purcell; p.7 right, Science Photo Library/James Stevenson; p.8, Science Photo Library/Fritz Henle; p.9, Science Photo Library/ NOAA; p.10/11, Corbis/Stocktrek; p.11, Corbis/Roger Ball; p.12, Panos Pictures/Trygve Bolstad; p.13, Panos Pictures/ Fred Hoogervorst; p.14/15, Frank Lane Picture Agency/ Colin Marshall; p.14, Frank Lane Picture Agency; p.16, Corbis/ Lester Lefkowitz; p.17, Corbis/NASA; p.18, Corbis; p.18, left, Science Photo Library/Chris Saltlberger; p.19, Corbis; p.20, Science Photo Library/2002 Orbital Imaging Corporation; p.21, Science Photo Library/NASA; p.21 right, Corbis/NASA; p.22, Corbis Sygma; p.23, Science Photo Library/Chris Saltlberger; p.24/25, Guy Motil/Corbis; p.24, Corbis/Bettmann; p.25, Corbis/Steve Starr; p.26/27, Corbis/ Galen Rowell; p.27, Frank Lane Picture Agency; p.28, Corbis/Jim McDonald; p.29, Corbis/Post and Courier; p.29 right, Corbis/Alan Schein; p.30/31, Corbis Sygma; p.30, Corbis/Annie Griffiths Belt; p.31, Corbis; p.32, Corbis Sygma; p.33, Corbis/Will & Deni McIntyre; p.34, Corbis/ Steve Starr; p.34 left, Corbis; p.35 Corbis Sygma; p.36/37, Corbis Sygma/Tramontina Gary; p.37, Corbis/Roger Ressmeyer; p.38, Science Photo Library/NASA/Goddard Space Flight Center; p.38 left, Corbis/John Van Hasselt; p.39, Corbis/Yan Arthus-Bertrand; p.40/41, Corbis Sygma; p.40, Corbis; p.41, Science Photo Library/Detlev Ravensway; p.42, Corbis/Kristin Royalty; p.43, Corbis; p.44, Corbis Sygma; p.45, Corbis/Stocktrek.

Cover photograph reproduced with permission of Associated Press

Every effort has been made to contact copyright holders of any material reproduced in this book. Any omissions will be rectified in subsequent printings if notice is given to the Publishers.

Contents

A Swirling Storm   4

Ocean Storms   6

Hurricane Science   14

Measuring Hurricanes   22

A Hurricane is Coming   26

A Hurricane Arrives   32

Going Inland   36

Fighting Hurricanes   40

Find Out More   44

Glossary   46

Index   48

Any words appearing in the text in bold, **like this**, are explained in the Glossary. You can also look out for some of them in the Stormy Words box at the bottom of each page.

A Swirling Storm

Imagine you are on the beach on a very windy day. Large waves crash onto the shore. Suddenly the sky fills with dark clouds. The winds blow more strongly and heavy rain starts to fall.

Winds and waves

The winds grow stronger and stronger. It is hard to walk against the wind. Tree branches, garbage cans, and roof shingles fly through the air. The sea level rises quickly. Huge waves **surge inland**. They smash into houses, wash away cars, and dump boats on the land. It is chaos everywhere. You are in the middle of a hurricane!

Wind speed

A hurricane can grow to hundreds of miles across. Near its center the winds can blow at more than 150 miles (240 kilometers) per hour.

Hurricane Bonnie ▷ arrives at Wilmington Beach, North Carolina, in 1998.

Stormy Words surge sudden rush

. . . what a hurricane looks like.

. . . what a **storm surge** is.

. . . what to do if a hurricane is coming.

Destruction!

The terrifying weather lasts for many hours. The hurricane destroys most things in its path. There is terrible flooding. The winds then start to die down. A few hours later, the sky is blue and the sea is calm. A trail of destruction is all that is left behind.

inland   part of a country away from the coast

Ocean Storms

Hurricane words

The word "hurricane" comes from the Caribbean god of storms, Hurican. The word **"typhoon"** comes from the Cantonese word tai-fung, meaning great wind.

A hurricane is a huge, swirling tropical storm. Inside are very strong winds and heavy rain. **Meteorologists** use the word "tropical" because hurricanes form over warm seas and oceans in the **tropics**.

A tropical storm becomes a hurricane when the winds blow faster than 73 miles (118 kilometers) per hour. In the center of a hurricane it is calm. This area is called the **eye**. Hurricanes move away from the tropics. When they hit colder land, they die away.

This map shows the areas that are ▽ most often hit by hurricanes.

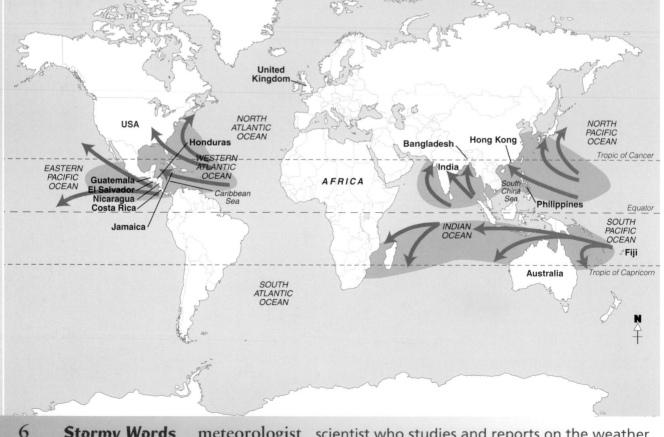

Stormy Words meteorologist scientist who studies and reports on the weather

Different names

Strong tropical storms in the Atlantic Ocean and the Caribbean Sea are called hurricanes. Storms that form in the western North Pacific Ocean and the China Sea are called typhoons. Storms in the Indian Ocean and Australia are called tropical **cyclones**. Everything we say about hurricanes is true for typhoons and cyclones, too.

The Great Storm

The Great Storm hit southern Britain in 1987 (above). Fifteen million trees were blown down.

◁ Hurricane Gilbert batters the Caribbean island of Jamaica in 1988.

typhoon   name given to a hurricane in the western North Pacific

Hurricane seasons

Hurricanes form at certain times of the year. These are called hurricane **seasons**. In the northern **hemisphere**, the hurricane season lasts from June to November. These are the summer and autumn months. By June, the sea has warmed up enough for hurricanes to develop. In the southern hemisphere, summer and autumn are between November and May. This is the hurricane season there.

Names to remember

Meteorologists give each new hurricane, typhoon, or tropical **cyclone** a name. This helps people to identify the hurricane when warnings are given. A new list of names, in alphabetical order, is started at the beginning of each year. The first hurricane's name starts with an A, the second with a B, and so on. About ten names are used up in the Atlantic region each year.

Regional names

The list of names for hurricanes in the Atlantic region is made up of boys' and girls' names. In the North Pacific region, animal and plant names are used.

◁ A **satellite** picture of Hurricane Ione (top) and Hurricane Kirsten (bottom).

cyclone   name given to a hurricane in the southern hemisphere

Hurricane Andrew

On August 17, 1992, a tropical storm began over the Atlantic Ocean. It was called Hurricane Andrew. By August 22 the storm was about 500 miles (800 kilometers) from the east coast of the USA. The next day it headed for the Bahamas. With winds blowing at more than 150 miles (240 kilometers) per hour, Hurricane Andrew moved straight toward Florida.

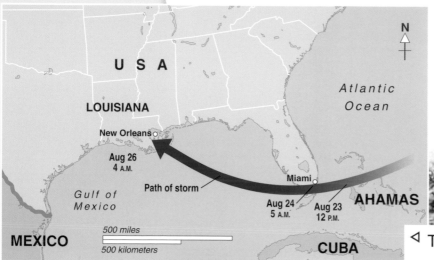

◁ This map shows the path of Hurricane Andrew.

Getting bigger

These three **satellite** pictures (right) show how Andrew developed as it moved westward. The eye has become much larger. The trails of clouds show that it is spinning faster.

Andrew hits land

Hurricane warnings were **broadcast** for the south of Florida. More than one million people left their homes. The **eye** of the storm hit the south of Miami. The sea level rose by 16 feet (5 meters). Huge waves flooded **inland**. Buildings were wrecked. Vehicles were flipped over. Trees were flattened. Gusts of wind were measured at more than 200 miles (320 kilometers) per hour.

Hurricane Andrew then moved into the Gulf of Mexico. It damaged oil rigs at sea. It hit the coast of Louisiana. This caused more destruction.

Homes flattened

Homes in this trailer park (below) were destroyed by Hurricane Andrew's winds.

eye   area in the center of a hurricane where the winds are calm

Bangladesh cyclones

Bangladesh is a country near the Indian Ocean. It suffers badly from flooding when a **cyclone** strikes. This is because most of the country is made up of a large **delta**. A delta is a low-lying area of many rivers that flow into the sea. As a cyclone moves through the Bay of Bengal, the heavy rains land on Bangladesh's delta. The delta floods easily.

Dangerous floods

In 1998, flooding was severe in Dhaka, the capital of Bangladesh. The water level in this street is more than 3 feet (1 meter) deep.

delta   wide, fan-shaped area of land where a river flows into the sea

Cyclone 2B

On April 29, 1991, a giant storm known as Cyclone 2B hit Bangladesh. The wind speeds reached 145 miles (235 kilometers) per hour. A wall of seawater, 20 feet (6 meters) high, **surged inland**. More than one million homes were destroyed. About 140,000 people died. Hurricane warnings were given out. But many people could not escape to higher ground.

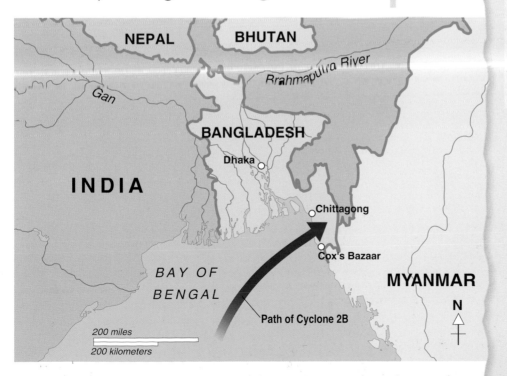

This map shows the path of Cyclone 2B heading for the Chittagong region of Bangladesh. ▽

NEPAL BHUTAN

Brahmaputra River

Gan

BANGLADESH

Dhaka

INDIA

Chittagong

Cox's Bazaar

BAY OF BENGAL

MYANMAR

N

Path of Cyclone 2B

200 miles

200 kilometers

Staple diet
These women are tending rice **paddies** in Bangladesh. If a cyclone destroys the paddy fields, it may lead to serious food shortages.

---

paddy   water-filled field used for growing rice

Hurricane Science

A hurricane is made up of a huge, swirling mass of clouds called **cumulonimbus** clouds. These clouds form into bands that are caught in the spiraling winds. The clouds then grow and rise. They start to spin around the **eye** of the hurricane.

Hundreds of thunderstorms and lightning flashes may be released. Very heavy rain and heat energy pours out. A typical hurricane is more than 300 miles (480 kilometers) across and more than 5 miles (8 kilometers) high.

Darwin devastated

One of the worst storms in Australia's history was **Cyclone** Tracy in 1974. It **devastated** the town of Darwin (below).

This is Fiji in the Pacific Ocean. Hurricanes form over warm seas like this.

Stormy Words   cumulonimbus   huge thunderclouds up to 6 miles (10 kilometers) high

Hurricane movement

Hurricanes develop over warm, tropical seas and oceans. They need the heat energy from the warm water to form and keep going. Hurricanes mainly move within and near the **tropics**. They may travel many thousands of miles and last for several weeks.

eye

surface of the sea

Spinning top

Imagine a hurricane as a spinning top. As it spins, it moves in a curving path. The cross-section above shows the direction in which a hurricane is spinning.

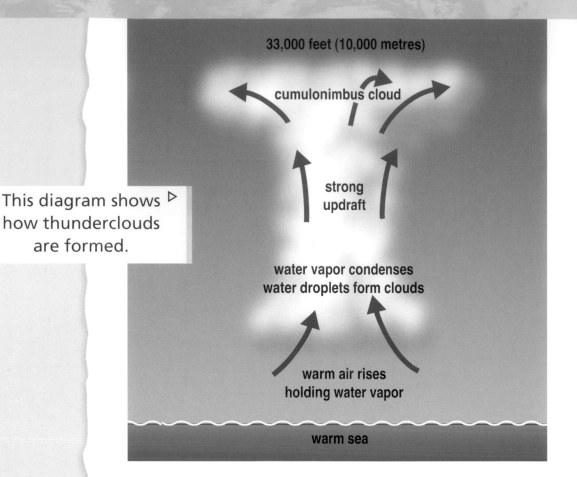

33,000 feet (10,000 metres)

cumulonimbus cloud

strong updraft

water vapor condenses
water droplets form clouds

warm air rises
holding water vapor

warm sea

This diagram shows ▷
how thunderclouds
are formed.

Storm energy

Scientists have worked out how much energy a hurricane makes in one day. It would produce enough electricity to run the lights of Las Vegas (right) for many years.

Hurricane formation

Before a hurricane can form, the water must be warmer than 80 °F (27 °C). Warm seawater heats the air above its surface. Warm air is good at holding **water vapor**. A lot of water **evaporates** from the sea into the air.

Forming clouds

Warm air normally rises upward. The rising air cools slowly. The water vapor **condenses** to form tiny water drops or ice crystals. The drops and crystals form clouds.

Towering storms

Heat from the water vapor keeps the air warm, and it continues to rise. This makes strong **updrafts**. They stop rising at about 33,000 feet (10,000 meters) above the surface. Then **cumulonimbus** storm clouds are formed.

Hurricane seedlings

A **seedling** is a group of thunderstorms. The **satellite** picture below shows a seedling over an ocean.

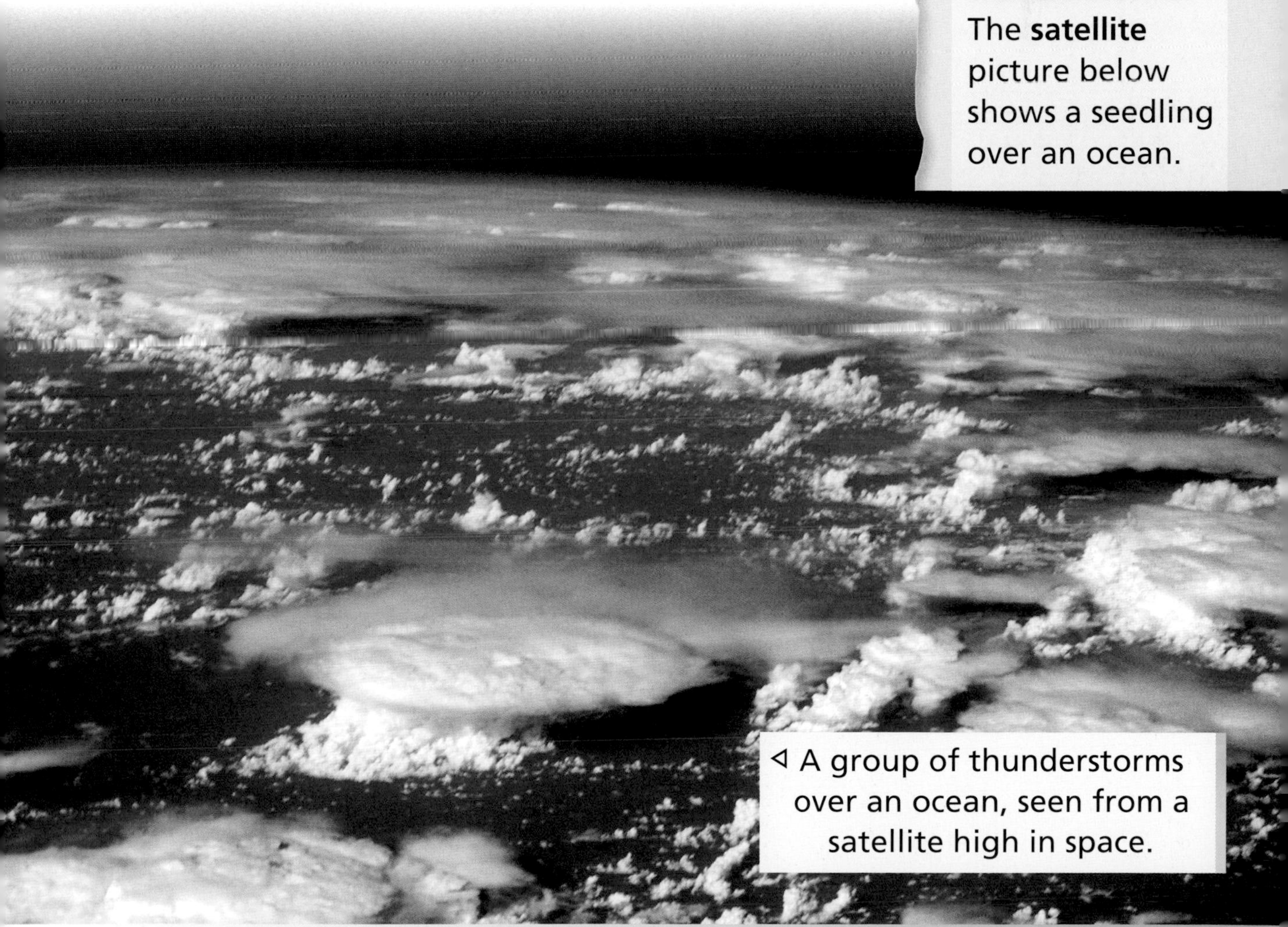

◁ A group of thunderstorms over an ocean, seen from a satellite high in space.

condense turn from gas into liquid

The eye of the storm

The **eye** is very small compared to the rest of the hurricane. Normally it is between 5 and 15 miles (8 and 24 kilometers) across. Toward the middle of a hurricane the winds get faster. But in the eye the winds are light.

From above, you can see straight through to the ocean beneath the hurricane. On the water's surface are giant waves. They are caused by the strong winds around the eye.

Hurricane hunting

Scientists search for hurricanes by sending out research planes. This photograph was taken in 1999. The aircraft is flying inside the eye of Hurricane Floyd.

△   The eye of Hurricane Isabel was photographed from the International Space Station in 2003.

The eye wall

Around the eye is a round wall of clouds up to 6 miles (10 kilometers) high. This is called the **eye wall**. The hurricane's fiercest winds are found there. The smaller the eye, the stronger the winds are. Severe thunderstorms in the eye wall often cause **tornadoes**. Tornadoes are spinning columns of air. Their winds are even stronger than hurricanes. Sometimes seabirds are trapped in the eye. They cannot fly though the violent winds in the eye wall.

Hurricane Camille

Mississippi was hit by Hurricane Camille in 1969. Some of the damage is shown below.

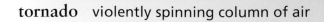

tornado   violently spinning column of air

Spinning storms

If a **seedling** thunderstorm forms near the **equator** it quickly dies away. This happens because of the way Earth **rotates**.

But at distances of more than 300 miles (483 kilometers) from the equator, the storm seedling begins to spin slowly. Winds do not blow in straight lines. They follow a curved path over Earth's surface. This is why storms begin to spin slowly and grow.

Spin direction

The picture above is of a storm south of Australia. It is spinning in a clockwise direction because it is in the southern hemisphere.

This diagram shows the curved path of winds over Earth's surface. ▽

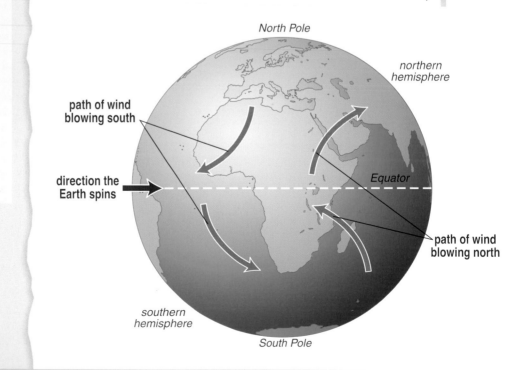

Stormy Words   rotate   twist round or turn

Storm to hurricane

Warm, moist air provides the energy that feeds a storm and makes it spin faster. If the winds reach 39 miles (62 kilometers) per hour, the storm is known as a tropical storm. When the winds reach 73 miles (118 kilometers) per hour, then it is a hurricane.

Tropical storms always rotate **counterclockwise** if they develop in the northern **hemisphere**. In the southern hemisphere they always rotate **clockwise**.

Dying storms
Most tropical storms and hurricanes die out before they hit land. The picture above shows a thunderstorm dying away.

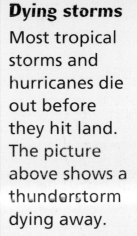

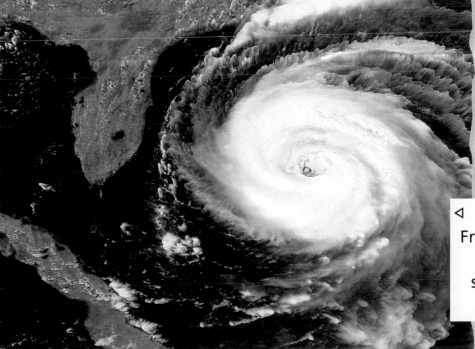

◁ This is Hurricane Fran in the northern hemisphere. It is spinning counter-clockwise.

counterclockwise   opposite to the direction that the hands of a clock move round

Measuring Hurricanes

Meteorologists measure the **intensity**, or strength, of hurricanes. They measure the speed of the winds. They also record how much damage the hurricane does when it reaches land.

Anemometer

The man below is measuring the wind speed using a hand-held **anemometer**.

The Saffir-Simpson scale

The **international** scale for measuring hurricanes is the Saffir-Simpson scale. There are five **categories**, as shown in the table below. Category 1 is the weakest or least intense. Category 5 is the strongest or most intense. The winds blow at the speeds listed for most of the time during the worst part of the storm.

National ▷ Hurricane Center in Florida.

The Saffir-Simpson scale

Category	Wind speed	Damage
1	73–94 miles per hour (118–152 kilometers)	Not much damage to buildings. Some trees fall. Trailer homes move. Some flooding on coasts.
2	95–109 miles per hour (153–176 kilometers)	Roofs, doors, and windows broken. Many trees fall. Piers damaged. Small boats swept ashore. Flooding of low-lying coasts.
3	110–129 miles per hour (177–208 kilometers)	Structures of buildings damaged. Trailer homes destroyed. Flooding up to 6 miles (10 km) **inland**.
4	130–154 miles per hour (209–248 kilometers)	Some roofs torn off and walls collapse. Beaches **eroded**. Large boats swept inland. Severe flooding up to 6 miles (10 km) inland.
5	more than 154 miles per hour (248 kilometers)	Some buildings destroyed by wind. Buildings near coast swept away by waves. Severe flooding up to 10 miles (16 km) inland.

international used by or to do with many different countries

Dangerous winds

A **category** 5 hurricane has wind speeds of more than 154 miles (248 kilometers) per hour around its **eye**. Some gusts can reach an incredible 200 miles (320 kilometers) per hour.

The violent winds whip up huge waves across the ocean. These waves can swamp even the biggest ships.

Fifi floods

Central America was hit by Hurricane Fifi in 1974. Twenty-five inches (63 centimeters) of rain fell in one day. Many houses, like these in Honduras, were surrounded by muddy water (below).

Storm surge

The **air pressure** in the center of a hurricane is very low. This means the air is pressing less heavily on the water below the hurricane's center than it is at its edges.

This makes the seawater rise underneath the hurricane. A large bulge or mound of water forms.

Sudden threat

As the hurricane winds sweep **inland,** the huge mound of water is carried on to the shore. This is called a **storm surge.** It is the most dangerous part of a hurricane. It can cause sudden flooding to low-lying areas.

Surge heights.
The picture above shows a storm surge crashing on to the coast of Palm Beach, Florida. The waves were 20 feet (6 meters) high.

A Hurricane is Coming

What is it like to be in the middle of a strong hurricane? How do you protect yourself? What happens to towns and cities? Let us see what happens when a **category** 4 hurricane forms and hits the southern coast of the United States.

Storms form at sea

A group of thunderstorms, a hurricane **seedling**, develops over the warm, tropical ocean. It is near the west coast of Africa. It shows up on images from weather **satellites**.

Hurricane path

The map below shows the path of the category 4 hurricane. It will travel over 1,000 miles (1,600 kilometers) to reach the U.S. It will take over a week to get there.

N

NORTH
AMERICA

USA

OHIO   WEST VIRGINIA
KENTUCKY
VIRGINIA
TENNESSEE
NORTH CAROLINA
GEORGIA
SOUTH CAROLINA

Bahamas

Atlantic
Ocean

AFRICA

Pacific
Ocean

Equator

2000 miles

2000 kilometers

SOUTH
AMERICA

This group of thunderstorm clouds could be the start of a new hurricane. ▷

satellite   device sent up into space by a rocket that orbits Earth

Gaining strength

The seedling begins to spin. It turns from a group of storms into one large spinning storm. In a few days it has grown into a tropical storm. It moves westward at 15 miles (24 kilometers) per hour. As it takes energy from the warm ocean, it spins faster. Finally, a small **eye** appears at its center.

Aircraft fly out to collect **data**. Winds near the eye are blowing at more than 100 miles (160 kilometers) per hour.

Shipping disaster

During World War II, a U.S. sailing fleet was hit by a **typhoon** in the Pacific Ocean. Three ships sank. Others were badly damaged, like the deck of this aircraft carrier (above).

data   information from an experiment, a survey, or stored on a computer

Preparing for a hurricane

About 36 hours before the hurricane is likely to hit land, a hurricane watch is **broadcast** on TV and radio. These are some of the things people do to prepare:

- fix wooden shutters or boards over windows,
- bring inside loose objects like garden furniture, garbage cans, and plant pots,
- check disaster supply kits (see left),
- stock up on food, first-aid, and drinking water.

These workers are fitting wooden boards across windows to prevent ▽ the glass from breaking.

Evacuation

Within 24 hours of a hurricane's expected arrival, a hurricane warning is broadcast. People living in its path are advised to **evacuate** their homes. There is no time to waste. They load up their cars and head for the nearest **evacuation route**.

Special shelters

In areas of the United States that are most at risk, there are special places where people can shelter. These are large, safe buildings, such as schools. Those who cannot leave, like the elderly, are usually moved there first.

Traffic jams often build up as everybody leaves at once. ▽

Follow the signs

In many places, local **officials** work out the best evacuation routes. This helps people to escape quickly to a safe place. Special signs (below) are put up to mark the route.

EVACUATION ROUTE

First signs

The hurricane is still far out at sea. It will not arrive for many hours. The wind is picking up and waves are crashing on to the shore. Gradually, the sky clouds over. Now it begins to rain and the wind is getting stronger. People check their **barometers**. The **air pressure** is falling quickly. The **eye** of the storm is on its way!

Hurricane Felix

Huge waves from Hurricane Felix crash into beach houses in Virginia, in 1995 (below). Some houses are built on **stilts** so that the water can run underneath.

This boat was carried inland by a storm surge caused by Cyclone Luis in 1995. ▽

Stormy Words   barometer   instrument that measures air pressure

Floods arrive

The sea level rises quickly as the **storm surge** arrives. Large waves pound over the shoreline. They carry cars, boats, and **debris** with them. Water rushes **inland**. Homes and shops are flooded. Buildings along the shore are wrecked by the waves.

Snake escape

When a storm surge causes flooding inland, even snakes are at risk. This Southern Pacific rattlesnake (below) will swim through the water to find dry land.

debris   bits and pieces of something broken or destroyed

A Hurricane Arrives

The most violent part of the storm, the **eye wall**, is right overhead. The wind is screaming. Rain is lashing down. Flashes of lightning streak across the dark sky.

Havoc!

Trees crash to the ground with their roots ripped out. The falling trees crush cars and houses. Traffic lights and streetlights swing wildly. Cars roll and trucks flip over. Roof shingles, sheets of metal, and patio furniture fly around.

Ripped apart

The photograph below was taken in the middle of a fierce hurricane. The dangerous winds have wrecked the canopy of this gas station.

Homeless
This couple look at the damage after Hurricane Hugo hit their home in South Carolina in 1989 (left).

The eye passes

Suddenly the winds start to die away. The sky clears and the sun shines. The hurricane seems to have gone. The **eye** of the storm has arrived, and there is calm for a while.

After only half an hour the winds start again. The eye has passed by. Houses are ripped apart. Apartment blocks lose their roofs. Glass crashes into the street. There is **havoc** everywhere.

havoc   great disorder and damage

The hurricane ends

It is twelve hours since the hurricane's **eye** passed. The wind has died down and it has stopped raining. The sea is calm. The sky is blue and the sun shines. Water in the streets slowly drains away.

Galveston

A hurricane destroyed the town of Galveston, Texas, in 1900. Most of the houses had been built of wood. Their **shattered** remains can be seen in the picture below.

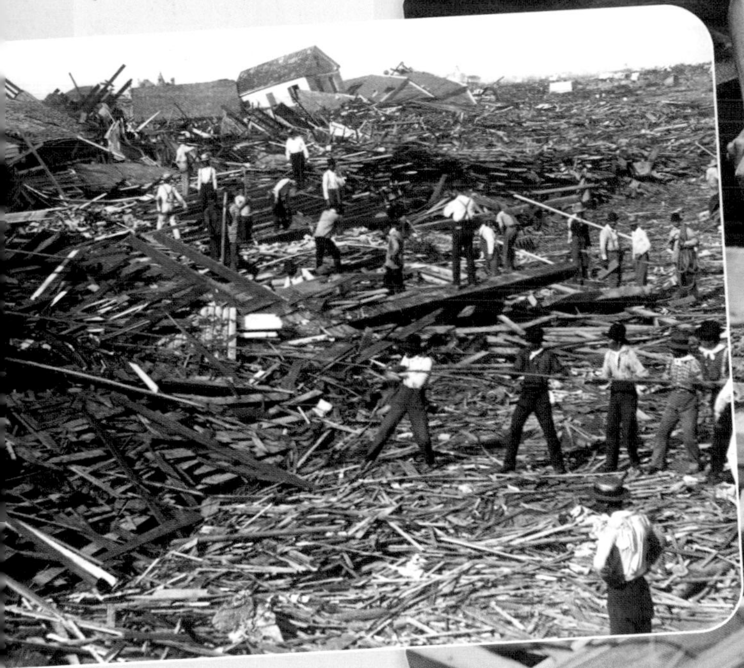

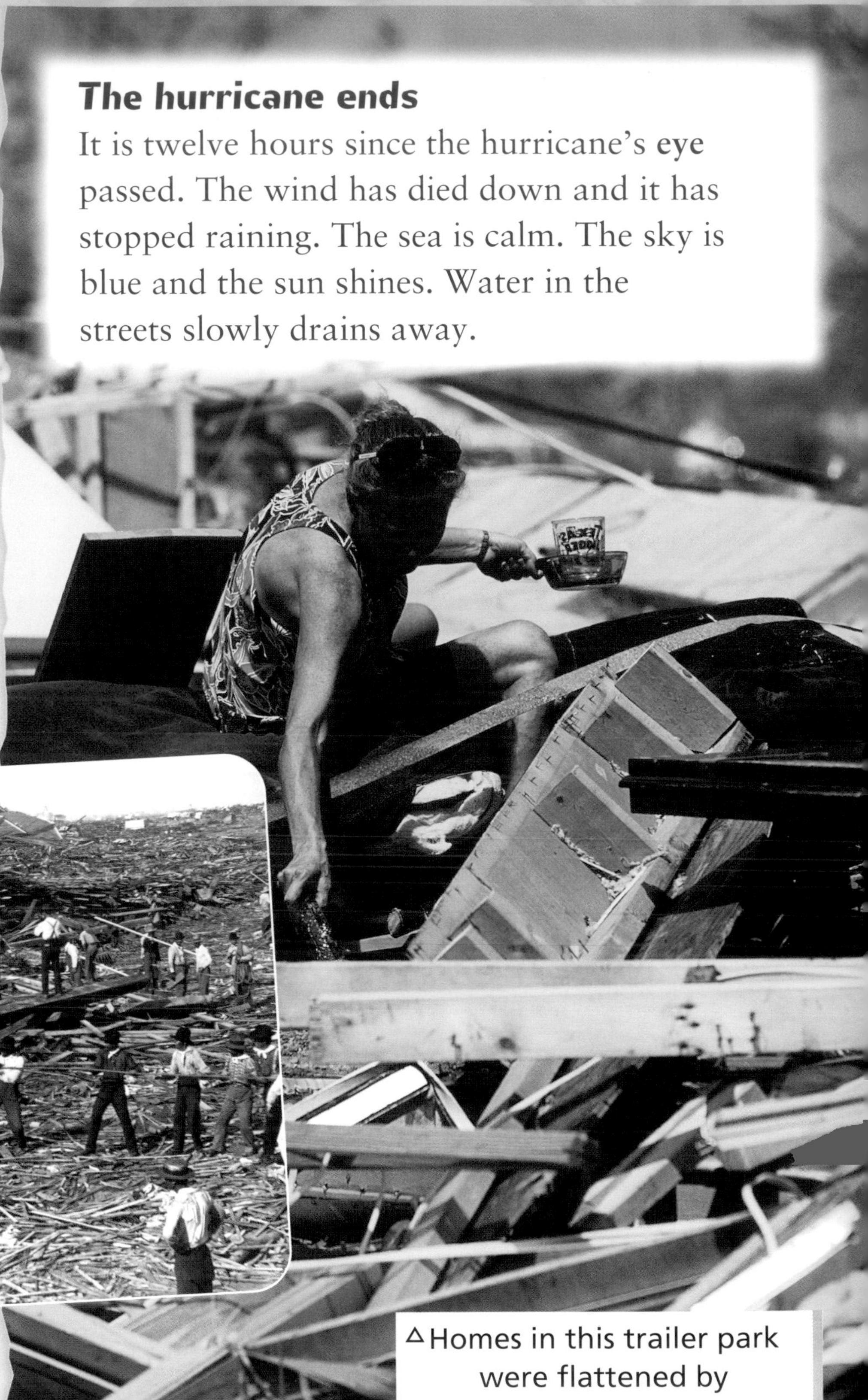

△ Homes in this trailer park were flattened by Hurricane Andrew in 1992.

Stormy Words shatter break suddenly into pieces

A terrible mess

People return to find **devastation** all around. The streets are full of mud and sand. Vehicles and boats lie in tangled heaps. Many people have lost their homes. The seawater has ruined their belongings.

Cleaning up

The hurricane caused so much destruction in only a few hours. It will take many months to clear up the mess. The winds have damaged electricity supplies, telephone lines, and water pipes. These services are restored as soon as possible. Builders start to rebuild damaged properties.

Dirty water

After a hurricane, water is often unsafe to drink. When Hurricane Andrew hit south Florida, freshwater supplies needed to be handed out (below).

devastation   destruction

Going Inland

After the hurricane has caused **havoc** on the coast, it starts to move **inland**. As it loses energy, it begins to die down slowly. Even so, the hurricane may last for several days. It can still do a lot more damage. The winds keep blowing strongly. Very heavy rain falls for hours on end.

Flash floods catch people without warning. Motorists are forced to leave their cars when water floods the engines. ▽

Flash floods

Streams and rivers fill up very quickly. They overflow their banks and flood low-lying areas. These are **flash floods**. They happen so quickly that people have no time to escape.

Rain mixes with earth to form mud. The mud slides down hillsides, causing even more damage. Then the winds start to calm down. Finally, the hurricane dies away.

Philippines mudslides

In 1991, **Typhoon** Yuna crossed the Philippines. A volcano **erupted** at the same time. Rain mixed with ash to form mudslides. Parts of these houses (below) have been swept away.

Hurricane Mitch

In October 1998, Hurricane Mitch hit Central America. It was a **category** 5 hurricane. The winds blew at more than 150 miles (240 kilometers) per hour. But it was the rain that did the most damage. Mitch moved slowly through the Caribbean. Over Honduras, in just one day, 25 inches (63 centimeters) of rain fell.

This **satellite** image shows Hurricane Mitch just off the coast of Honduras. ▽

Staying safe

These survivors escaped from a mudslide in Nicaragua. It was caused by Hurricane Mitch. They are wearing face masks to protect them from the **fumes** from dead bodies.

Floods and mudslides

The rains caused terrible floods. Rivers grew into raging **torrents**. They swept away houses, people, and animals. Food crops were destroyed. Hillsides collapsed causing powerful mudslides.

Devastation

Hurricane Mitch left behind a trail of destruction. Roads and bridges had been washed away. This made it very hard for the rescue and medical teams to reach survivors.

Guanaja island

The island of Guanaja in Honduras was **devastated** by Mitch (below). The hurricane also wrecked Honduran crops of bananas, coffee, and sugarcane.

torrents   rushing streams of water

Fighting Hurricanes

Weather satellites

Weather satellites can be used to track hurricanes. This one (below) sends back photographs of the **atmosphere** every half hour.

Scientists need as much information as possible to help them **forecast** a hurricane.

Hurricane forecasting

Satellite images show the exact position of **seedlings**, tropical storms, and hurricanes.

Aircraft fly into storms. They collect information about wind speeds and **air pressure**. The **data** is fed into computers. The computers work out where the hurricane will hit.

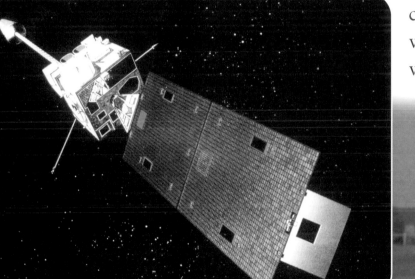

Hurricane research

Hurricanes are difficult to predict. They often land in places where they are not expected.

Researchers try to find out why hurricanes change direction. They study measurements from hurricanes in the past. They find out how sea temperatures change when hurricanes pass over them. They try to link the pattern of hurricanes with other extreme world weather patterns.

This truck is a hurricane chaser. It uses **Doppler radar** to measure wind speeds.

▽

Seen from space
A giant thunderstorm, like this one below, could be the first sign that a new hurricane is about to be born.

Doppler radar   instrument that can detect objects and measure wind speeds

Getting safer

More and more people are choosing to live in hurricane areas. This means that about 15 percent of the world's population is at risk. But the number of people killed and injured by hurricanes is getting fewer. This is because of better **forecasting** and warnings. People are also better prepared about what to do if a hurricane strikes.

△ Members of the U.S. Air Force track the progress of Hurricane Isabel in 2003.

Controlling hurricanes

We cannot stop hurricanes, but is it possible to control them? If so, it might reduce the damage that they cause. Weather experts have been working on some ideas to weaken hurricanes or make them change direction. But there is still much to learn.

Hurricane resistant
Tall buildings must be strengthened to withstand hurricane-force winds. These skyscrapers in Hong Kong (below) are designed to stay standing when a **typhoon** hits.

Find Out More

Organizations

National Hurricane Center

The NHC keeps watch on hurricanes in the eastern Pacific and Atlantic. The Center issues forecasts, watches, and warnings. The NHC offers education programs for people affected by hurricanes worldwide.
To find out more, contact them at this address:

**National Hurricane Center
11691 S.W. 17th Street, Miami, Florida
33165-2149**

Books

Chambers, Catherine. *Disasters in Nature: Hurricanes.* Chicago: Heinemann Library, 2000.
Steele, Christy. *Nature on the Rampage: Hurricanes.* Chicago: Raintree, 2004.

World Wide Web

To find out more about hurricanes you can search the Internet. Use keywords like these:

- hurricane +[country]
- "storm surge"
- Bangladesh +cyclones

You can find your own keywords by using words from this book. The search tips opposite will help you find useful websites.

Search tips

There are billions of pages on the Internet. It can be difficult to find exactly what you are looking for. These tips will help you find useful websites more quickly:

- Know what you want to find out.
- Use simple keywords.
- Use two to six keywords in a search.
- Only use names of people, places, or things.
- Put double quote marks around words that go together, for example "eye wall."

Where to look

Search engine

A search engine looks through millions of website pages. It lists all the sites that match the words in the search box. You will find the best matches are at the top of the list, on the first page.

Search directory

A person instead of a computer has sorted a search directory. You can search by keyword or subject and browse through the different sites. It is like looking through books on a library shelf.

Glossary

air pressure   force of air pressing down on the Earth

anemometer   instrument for measuring the force of the wind

atmosphere   layer of gases that surround the Earth

barometer   instrument that measures air pressure

broadcast   send information over the radio or television

category   group or class of things

clockwise   direction that the hands of a clock move round

condense   turn from gas into liquid

counterclockwise   opposite to the direction that the hands of a clock move round

cumulonimbus   huge thunderclouds up to 6 miles (10 kilometers) high

cyclone   name given to a hurricane in the southern hemisphere

data   information from an experiment, a survey, or stored on a computer

debris   bits and pieces of something broken or destroyed

delta   wide, fan-shaped area of land where a river flows into the sea

devastate   cause great destruction

devastation   destruction

Doppler radar   instrument that can detect objects and measure wind speeds

engineer   person who designs and builds things like machines, roads, and bridges

equator   imaginary line around the middle of Earth

erode   wear away by action of water, wind, or ice

erupt   sudden force of gas, fire, and ash through Earth's surface

evacuate   leave a place of danger

evacuation route   path to follow to reach a safe place

evaporate   turn from liquid into gas

eye   area in the center of a hurricane where the winds are calm

eye wall   wall of tall clouds around the eye of a hurricane

flash floods   quickly developing floods

forecast   give information about something that might happen

fumes   harmful gases and vapor

havoc   great disorder and damage

hemisphere   one half of Earth

inland   part of a country away from the coast

intensity   strength

international   used by or to do with many different countries

meteorologist   scientist who studies and reports on the weather

official   person employed by a public body or organization

paddy   water-filled field used for growing rice

rotate   twist round or turn

satellite   device sent up into space by a rocket that orbits Earth

season   time of year with typical weather

seedling   group of thunderstorms that may turn into a hurricane

shatter   break suddenly into pieces

stilts   raised legs

storm surge   sudden rise in sea level that happens as a hurricane approaches land

surge   sudden rush

tornado   violently spinning column of air

torrents   rushing streams of water

tropics   area of the world, near the equator, where the weather is warm

typhoon   name given to a hurricane in the western North Pacific

updraft   rising air

water vapor   water in the form of a gas

Index

aid 35, 39
air 16–17, 21
air pressure 25, 30, 40
aircraft 18, 27, 40
animals 31
Atlantic Ocean 7, 10
Australia 7, 14, 20

Bahamas 10
Bangladesh 12–13
birds 19
Britain 7

Caribbean 6–7, 22, 38
Caribbean Sea 7
China Sea 7
clouds 14–15, 17, 19
computers 40
crops 39
cyclones 7, 9, 12–14, 17

damage 4–5, 11, 23, 27, 33,
    35, 37, 38–39
Darwin, Australia 14
disaster plans 28
Doppler radar 41

energy 14–16, 21, 27, 36
equator 20
evacuation 29
eye walls 19, 32
eyes of hurricanes 6, 10–11,
    14, 18–19, 24, 27, 30, 33–34

Fiji 15
floods 12–13, 24, 31, 36–37,
    39
Florida 10–11, 23, 25, 35
forecasts 40, 42

Galveston, Texas 34
Gulf of Mexico 11

Honduras 24, 38–39
Hurricane Andrew 10–11,
    34–35
Hurricane Camille 19
Hurricane Fifi 24
Hurricane Hugo 8, 33

Hurricane Mitch 38–39
hurricane names 9
hurricane seasons 8
hurricane seedlings 17, 20,
    26–27, 40
hurricane sizes 14–15, 18
hurricane speeds 23, 27
hurricane survival 28, 42
hurricane watch 28
hurricane-resistant buildings
    43

Indian Ocean 7
Internet 44–45

Louisiana 11

measuring hurricanes 22–23
meteorologists 6, 9, 22–23
Miami, Florida 11
Mississippi 19
mudslides 37, 39

National Hurricane Center,
    Florida 23
Nicaragua 38
northern hemisphere 8, 21

Pacific Ocean 7, 24, 27
Philippines 37

rain 4, 6, 14, 24, 30, 34, 36–39
research 18, 41
rice paddies 13

Saffir, Herbert 23
Saffir-Simpson scale 23
satellites 26, 40
shelters 29
Simpson, Robert 23
snakes 31
southern hemisphere 8, 21
storm surges 25, 31

thunderstorms 14, 17, 19,
    20–21, 26, 41
tornadoes 19
tropical storms 6–7, 10, 21,
    27, 40

tropics 6, 15
typhoons 6–7, 9, 27, 37, 43

updrafts 17

volcanoes 37

warnings 11, 13, 42
water supplies 35
water temperature 16, 41
waves 4, 11, 18, 23–25, 30–31
winds 4–6, 10–11, 13–14,
    18–25, 27, 30, 32–33,
    35–38, 40, 43